PREFACE

This is English-Translated Verse Version of best selected poems of Sir Rabindranath Tagore, on Death and beyond death. 72 short and long poems [68 of them 1st time] translated into English, specially selected on the death-related themes only, representing all issues, reality of Death, fear of death, people's helplessness against this inevitable incidence, human endeavors to face it, fight against it, reconcile with it, and also overcome it, through a multiple approaches prescribed in religious, theosophical, philosophical, and scientific interpretation of the creative process of the Universe and living entities. There are some more poems, songs of Tagore, and his other writings, including his Books on Religion. This great poet, only poet on Earth published 4000+ Poems, composed 3000+ songs. He and his family were an early production of Indian Renaissance that originated in Kolkata and flourished in 19th Century.

Tagore is the only writer of total human history who has 217 books of original creation, published in his name, of which 52 are books of Poems, published 29 prose dramas, 14 full-size novels, 17 poetic dramas , 6 dance-dramas, 5 books of collections of his Short Stories Auto-biographies are 3, Books on tour diaries of various countries are 9, his though-provoking letters are printed in 2 books , he wrote biographies of 5 great persons including Lod Jess Christ and Lord Buddha, Mahatma Gandhi. His books on religion are 6, his Essay books on Nationalism, Internationalism , Indian cultural and Socio-Economical issues are 2, books on Language, Literature, phonetics, Universe, and Msc. are 17, translated Macbeth of Shakespeare [partly] and Dohas of Kavir. He was a great painter, great singer, composer, an actor in his own dramas, President of a new religious sect, called Bramha-Samaj based upon the Doctrines of Upansads. He was also a great philanthropist and Educationist, who established new educational system and his own school, and college, which is now a big University under the National Government of India.

These thematically well-selected 71 Poems of Tagore, on the subject of Death and Beyond Death, have been divided in 12 thematic Categories in 12 Chapters, which deals with all the issues, from the pains-losses-sufferings and pathetic memories of the diseased person, near and dear, lover and beloved, gradually taking readers to higher platform of thoughts and realization of Creative process, the Creator's designs, transformation of forms and energy, keeping total aggregate same and unchanged, nothing is lost in the Universe of the Supreme creator and sustainer of this created systems and entities[I called then Solace-Systems]

In Christian belief buried people wait for the final day of their judgements, so the soul with individual entity continues intact till that final day. Similar is the thoughts and believes in the Islamic faiths.

The Science says, forms to energy, energy to forms, all these continuous changes do not affect the total energy; and thus in this recycling process nothing is actually lost.

2

Rabindranath Tagore :The Death and the Deathless

Some people takes solace with believes in liberation [an emancipation from continuous Recycling through births-deaths process] a Buddhist and also a Hindu thought, some paths of solace people finds in the belief in Re-birth [mainly a Hindu belief; and devotees of most faiths find final solace in faithful surrender of all matters to His pleasure, and at His feet. Some theosophical belief of non-perishability of Soul [Aatma], argued by the Upanisads to Geeta, tallies partially with Tagore's own experience of seeing inner-self outside his own physical body {Poem No.58}, and his one experience of a sort of resurrection experience as narrated by him in Poem No. 57, and at the last phase of his life, he totally denied death as the ends of the Entities [vide poems no. 54 to 62] a final conviction that the Creator, processed out after 1450 Crores of years after the Big Bang, giving Humans, the only creature enter into perusal and de-codification of His Universe, it's creative process, tried to understand their Creator.

Tagore believed that it is the God [the invisible creative force, having 3 great attributes, "Sat-chit-Ananda" [**permanency-intellects-creative-urges**] is involved in a creative program [out of His grace or pleasure] and proceeded with such an evolution-program, that someday, His off-springs will duly realize and interact with Him, with love and dignity . As in real life, a father or a mother [who brought any child on Earth] want to get their first great pleasure, when their off-springs first distinctly identify their parents and call them "father" or " mother" as the case may be. Such is the relation of mankind with the Universal Creator or the Supreme One, whom we call in various names, manners and may be in a very wrong manners [as ordinary persons have no greater brain power to conceive anything beyond an Anthropometric God.

Tagore's God is One, invisible but feel-able who always approaching to make Himself fully revealed and mingled with. Out of His own pleasure, out of His own love for the mankind has been coming down to us. And similarly, the mankind is the only product of God, who had been trying utmost to discover who is that ONE, and the mankind is also in a march to meet and mingle with their Creator. This mutual love-relation is reflected in Tagore's poems vide]specially Poem No. 51 to 56 [Chapter-11 : Re-Union]...I felt the greatest need of this critical time of human face, fighting the CODID-19, with unthinkable numbers of daily deaths, to reach to global population through English translation of Tagore's poems relevant now.

I have also provided BEST Singer's Link in YouTube so that you can listen all the melodious tunes, Tagore has given to all those song-poems so far sung. If you have no time to read, please listen Tagore's tunes of high serenity. Type the fist line of all shot-poems in English Script in You-Tube and you can enjoy beautiful tunes of best singers.

The Great Qualities of expressing his thoughts, specially in poetic language and more so, by his self-created uncommon tunes**, will definitely be enchanting and appealing to**

4

swollen-up souls, who are going to meet death of himself or of his near and dear one, inevitable.

Death being a must event of our birth, it will be a unique pleasure to see how a great visionary like Tagore, expressed his own experience in his 80-years of life, taking all the pains of most untimely deaths of his beloved wife and all his five children. I hope you will surely get whatever you need to realize the acts of deaths, pathos associated, people's multiple faiths to win over the death-threats and post-death solaces from different faiths, and philosophical, theosophical and other ideas/values created by global humans so far for their own benefit. See wherein do you find yourself fit and comfortable.

Never-the-less, before any one of us shall die, may it be a good courtesy to pay a final Salutation to the God, the Creator, and to this Mother Earth on whose lap we spent our days in a life-form, and see a sample, how Tagore did it in his Poem at Serial No. 54 to God, and his Last Salutation to this Mother Earth by his poem at Serial No. 3 of this collection.

Because of the difficult task of transferring the beauty and the fragrance of any exceptionally blossomed poetic expressions, even in the same language by the same poet [as Leonardo Da Vinci failed to re-create Monalisa twice], so it is more true to do this by using another language [specially of different phonetic group], and hence a very few of Tagore's poems and other writings have been translated and could be brough before the eyes, ears and hearts of global humans .

Rabindranath Tagore :The Death and the Deathless

This first efforts to translate Tagore's Poems in the English Verse Form, taken up by this over-anxious translator, using Word-to-Word & Line-to-Line translation formula to remain deadly committed to the highest possible accuracy, despite not finding exact synonyms in English dictionaries. But at least, in this current days of massive death-threats brought by COVID-19, this carefully selected thematically poems on Deaths and beyond, titled **" The Death and the Deathless"** may quite helpful to the global population, and shall surely provide, 'THE SOLACE OF LIVING A LIFE AND ALSO THE SOLACE WHILE MEETING THE ENEVITABLE INCIDENCE CALLED DEATHS'.

Seeking forgiveness for all mistakes,

Sukumar Das, MA[Double]
Compiler, Translator & Publisher,
of the English Version of these selected poems on
"**The Death and the Deathless**"
▪▪

The Death and the Deathless

INDEX OF CONTENS
Part-1 : On the reality of Death

CHAPTER-1
[The Fact of death & death-pangs on Earth]

CHAPTER-2
[Eternal cries-not to let anyone pass away]

CHAPTER-3
[Poems of painful memories]

CHAPTER-4
[Searching the Demised Beloved]

8

PART-II
[Towards Realization of Death-less-ness]

CHAPTER-5 [At His Feet : Solace System-1]
[Tolerating death-pains with total **faiths in Lord** of this Creation and Scientific explanation, that despite changes in mass, the Aggregate Energy of the Universe, remains the same]

CHAPTER -6 [Solace-System-2]
[Accepting Death- **as an Act of God** :
                Another Basic Solace]

CHAPTER-7
[Bravery to face Death -Solace-System -3]
[Fight to deafer the Deaths & sufferings]

CHAPTER-8
[Overcoming the fear of death: Solace-System-4]

CHAPTER-9
[Re-birth : Solace-System-5]
[Consolations through faiths in Re-birth]

CHAPTER-10
[Liberation; Solace System-6]
[A feeling of liberation from the Cycle of births]

CHAPTER-11 [Solace-System-7]
[A feeling of re-union with the Creator]

CHAPTER-12 [Solace System -8]
[Defying the Deaths & it's Consequences]

        ****

PART-1 : ON DEATH
CHAPTER-1
[The Fact of death & death-pangs on Earth]

1.Death-Life-Continuum

With Millions and billions of deaths,
Big small and tiny deaths, laughing and playing
On the surface of this Earth;
This Earth is running through the ever blue sky,
Being accompanied by deaths,
her eternal celestial trip;
The Axis of Earth is the Axis of deaths' passages,
This Globe is a playground of deaths always.

The length of years,
we thing we are living on Earth,
Passing through process of deaths,
is the real truth.
We have been dying, in every particles of time.
Being the living corpse,
residing in the abode of deaths,
Can't differentiate between the life and deaths .

No escape, let's the fill up your heart,
with delighted cheer-fullness,
And seeing this Earth's festival of deaths, endless;
At whose invitation, we are here festive in grandeur,
Resounding the horizon with painful clamor ?

Whatever we call a life, [I sweath]
We actually denote a death,
To us the death is not thus an alien,
Hold it's hand and embrace then.
****

[Written by the poet at his 17th years of age]

Rabindranath Tagore :The Death and the Deathless
2. End of our dream-full slumber, my dear

In what dream-full slumber,
we were, alluring so far !
Time is up for getting up
and going forward-
Before I depart, tell me your last few word.

At this moment, give me something,
Not looking back at me again;
To make my pains of separation a bit alluring,
To engrave this moment in my heart always,
At this moment of separation of bond and ties
Just for once, see my face with tearful eyes.

With wink-less gaze, this Morning Star,
Shall rise up in my next life's dawns,
Beaming lights to a distant sky,
where I may stay
In the long period of separation-day,
Till end of my life's evening-
Till my last moments' departing crying .

The lost diamonds [of our priceless love]
Shall remain strung as a garland
in my dreams,
Oh, my depressed beloved,
by own hands of yours,
Now, open my get-away gate's doors .
....

3. MY MOTHER EARTH-TAKE MY LAST SALUTATION
[Aaj aamar pranati graham karo Prithibi]
[3RD POEM OF "PATRAPUT" BOOK OF VERSE-1935]

Today, thou accept my Salutation, Oh, The Earth
Paying my last regards, laying down on the
Alter of my Life's Sun-set.
Most powerful thou, as enjoyed by the mighty ones
Reversable is your mood,
between the soft and harsh,
By nature you are a mixture
of masculinity and femininity;
You are swinging human lives
between unbearable contradictions.

While your right hand pours down nectar
Your left hand shatters the drinking vessel
Your pleasure-play-ground resounded
by your high-volume satires;
The braves, who deserve great living,
are made to fight unachievable targets
Everything beneficial is made hard to pay,
You don't show empathy to anyone so deserving
In your our trees and plants, hidden are the scars,
of their constant fights.

They wear their victory garlands in the forms
of grains and flowers.
In the land and sea, everywhere laid your
merciless war fields,
There the deaths only declare the messages of
victory over the forces of life .

On the foundation stone of brutality,
raised the victory gates of civilization-

15

Rabindranath Tagore :The Death and the Deathless

Any faulty failure has to be paid up fully
                    by total devastations !

Danavas@ dominated your early history-
            with undefeatable powers,
They were rude, barbarians, devoid of senses ;
            Their fingers were blunt,
    incapable of creating of art and beauties
With clubs and fire-stands, devasted all,
            till the Oceans and Mountains,
The fearful nightmares of fire and flames
            maddened the skies.
    In the kingdom of life-lessness,
                they were the overlords,
They had absolutely blind jealousy on Life.

Devas [the Gods] appeared in the later age,
Hymns were uttered to suppress the Danavas
    The despotism ended in tranquil
You sat over thy green verses rearing the mankind.
    The new dawn smiled over the
                peaks of Eastern mountains,
        On the shores of Western Seas,
                Lady Evening landed,
With a jar of Peace on her head.

The Danavas bowed their heads
                with chains in hands,
    Still that primeval barbarism
                imbibed in your history
Suddenly imports chaos in the settled systems
    Appearing out of the dark holes
                of your secret nature
    Suddenly scrawled out in zigzag ways,

In thy veins, that madness, remains imbibed .
Devine Hymns resounding the sky, airs and
forests,
In the days and in the nights,
In the tunes both loud and melodious.
Yet, from the hells of your crude heart,
those devil snakes
Raising their poisonous face to bite,
And thou hurting your own noble beings,
those hunters.
And burning down your own creations.

On thy feet laid on the Devine
and devilish Altar,
in recognition of your greatness
in both Beauty and fierce

Today, through this salutation,
I lay down the portrait of my life,
With imprinted signs of wounds
and scars all over .
Oh, thou, the great but secret source of
both Life and Death,
Under your covered surface of clay and soil,
I do touch that and imbibe
in my body and soul.

On thy uncountable ages and spheres
The buried bodies of countless humans
are heaped up.
I am also to put down there some
ashes of mine
The end result of my life's happiness and pains,

17

Rabindranath Tagore :The Death and the Deathless

Leaving all, inside your black-hole vanishing
all names, forms and fames
Within the soundless grand cover of
clay and dust.

Seized and barricaded by the unsurpassable
mountain ranges,
Flying invisibly though the wide sky-path,
Oh, the meditating Earth in the great silence
of the snowy picks,
Blue water's ceaseless waves in the oceans,
keeping your voice eloquent,
Thou a beauty with food and waters,
fearful where devoid of gains.
At one side, your green-fields filled with
ripen paddy on bent up plants,
The pleasing Sun-rays sip up the daily dews
fallen on the grain-flowers,
Sponging by the soft scarfs of rays.
And the setting Sun, sends soundless message
to the waves of greeneries,
" I am so delighted".

Somewhere else, in your waterless fruitless
terrific pink desert
With scattered skeletons of the dead animals,
and ghostly dances of mirages-
In Baishakh [mid-summer]-seen thy cyclones
clinching the horizon
With the beaks of the lightening,
Diving down as a black hawk,
The whole sky roared up like the angry lion
with raised manes,

And with it's flapping tail,
  breaking the branches, causing pandemonium-
        Hopelessly fatigued tall trees,
            fell down on their ribs.
The covers of the cottages,
            flied with the fierce storms
Like the imprisoned bandits.
        whose iron-chains fully broken.

    On the other hands, in Falguna [Springs]
        I saw your warm southern breeze
        Spread away the secret soliloquies
            of love and separation
Through fragrance from flowers of Mango trees.
The silvery plate of the Moon overflowed down
The sparkling foams of Devine drinks so frenzy
The murmuring sounds of the forests lost
        tolerance due to desperate flow of winds
And suddenly burst into elated roaring waves.

Tenderly thou, ferocious thou,
                very old but young for ever,
    From the fathomless beginning of creation,
        out of the fire-floated bed of creative altar,
    On a fine morning of an uncountable past,
    Along the long road of your moving chariot,
            You have crossed and passed
    At the end of hundreds of broken history and
            their lost-meaning remnants,
Without any feeling of pains, you left behind
        anything of your abandoned past
    Countless layers of sheer forgetfulness.

    Oh, midwife of the animal world, you have put us

Rabindranath Tagore :The Death and the Deathless

In the pigeon-cases of small fragmented time-frames
Within which we are to end our playing slots,
Within which, all our achievements ends.

To-day I have not come before you
with any illusory prayer;
So long all these days and nights,
the garland of words I stringed,
For which I will never demand from you
my deathless remembrance,
In your circular runway, around the Sun,
for millions and billions of years,
All those endlessly fragmented times
that arises and passes away,
If in any small parts within those fragmented time,
If ever I occupied even one single seat of duty,
And paid up for its true value,
And led to fruition, my life's any single fruitful part,
If I had achieved that success with extreme pains,

Then give me on my forehead
one single Tilak-mark of your watery clay,
That momentary sign shall also
get washed away,
In that night, when all signs vanish
into the final unknown cave.
Oh, my indifferent mother Earth,
Before you finally forget me
On thy cruel and unkind feet
I hereby lay down my last salutation.
....
Composed on :16th October-1935
....
@ Danavas [Dare-devil-hominids of ancient time]

20

4.In this birthday of mine,
seemingly I do not exist

In this birthday of mine,

It seems, I do not exist,

I beg to get from my friends

Still on Earth who do persist .

Only through the touches of their hands ,

All those last drops of earthly affections-

I shall take that as my ultimate

propitious gift of a kind

I wish to depart with those

last blessings of mankind.

My carry-bag is empty today;

I have given out and away

All that I had whatsoever, as yet ;

As a return gift, if I could ever get-

Some love, affection and forgiveness

And I must take those as their kindness

When I board the ferry boat[for a journey endless]

To land on the shore of

end-festival of speechlessness.

****

5. ETERNAL FUTILITY

Only to come and only to go,
        only to float with the flow
Only in light and darkness,
        some laughter and cries !
Only to have a meet,
        only to get a touch, then go !
Only to cry, looking back while going forth !

Only with new high hopes, going far and far.
Leaving behind false and lost up hopes, ever.

Having endless desires, with strength inapt,
The intense efforts, yielding impaired result,

Boarding broken boat, to sail across the ocean,
Emotions crying for expression, words limp often.

Heart to heart communications
        remains half-complete,
If half of the word is told, untold
        remains the other half;
In shyness, in fear of risk, in anxiety,
        in half-grown trust,
Alas, only to end up a life,
        tasting a half-grown love !
****

6. On the bank of Roopnaarayan river
[Roopnarayaner kule jege uthilaam]
LEKHA -11THE POEM OF THE BOOK

On the bank of river Roopnarayan,
[current of energy which gives birth of forms]
I emerged
And realized that this Creation
Is not a flowery dream at all.

By the alphabets of bloods, I saw
My existence was being painted.
I understood that I exist
By getting blows after blows
By tasting pains and sufferings.

Truth is something, ever, quite hard,
I happened to love that hardship-ness,
As the Truth never deceives or pretends .

Till your death, life is an ascetic austerity,
Practiced with pains,
To pay the tremendously high price of truth,
[through pains and sufferings]
Death will ever come to rid you off,
From your unpaid debts.

****

CHAPTER-2
[Eternal cries :not to let anyone passes away]

7. I WILL NOT ALLOW YOU TO GO
[Jete naahi dibo]"GOLDEN BOAT"-book -1893]

It was a mid-day, car was waiting at my door ,
Autumn Sun getting gradually fierce more and more.
....
Got to go for a distant land, at my work-place,
  As vacation is over, Luggage packed up,
 Came to take leave from my little daughter,
Sitting there at a corner of our outer door,
Listless was seen my daughter, aged four,
Boldly announced, so-
" I will not let you to go".
....
Listening in those boastful words of a child, throwing
Satire-full smiles to ignore her forceful affection,
Reality of life really snatched me away,.......
My defeated daughter, with her tears in eyes,
Remained fixed on the door-step, like a statue.
Staring at her, I set out, wiping out my own tears.

While travelling I saw on both sides of my roads,
The Autumn paddy fields,
                bent down with heavy crops,
Taking a Sun-bath, and the indifferent forest-trees,
Dividing the highways althrough, looking whole day,
Down on their depressed shadows.
Angry currents flowing through
                the swollen up Ganges *.
The white tiny pieces of clouds,
                like new born calves,
Happily, sucking mother's milk, sleeping scattered
Over the blue sky. Under the scorching Sun,

Rabindranath Tagore :The Death and the Deathless

Seeing the Earth, lying exposed, till the horizons,
With all tiredness of countless ages,
I could but only to breath out a very long sigh.

Saw sunk down in the deepest sorrows, the sky,
And the whole Earth. Whatever distance travelled,
I only heard this heart-breaking single tune,
'I will never let you go!'. From this end of the Earth,
Till all ends of this dark blue sky,
Resounding all over, since the endless ages,
This eternal cry, 'Shall not allow to go'.
Even mother Earth, a tiny grass, on her lap,
Crying at her best - 'Shall not allow to go'.!
....
In his endless universe,
        covering the Earth and Heavens,
The oldest words and extremely deepest cry,
Surely sounding the eternal cry-
'Shall not allow to go'. But alas !
Still you need to allow, and let all go.

Such is happening from the beginning of time,
And shall happen, till the entire stream of creation
Ends up totally in Ocean of dissolution !
Expanding their anxious arms, with burning eyes,
All are calling " No, no, not giving you any way to go.'
Despite that, all go away, in speed and roar ,
Filling up this shores of Earth with fearful clamor.
....
 With pale face tearful eyes,
At every wink of time, lost of pride ever, still love, by
no means, surrenders, rebellious she,
 speaks choked voice,
        'Shall never let you go'.
    After all the defeats, always shy-less she repeats,
            "Whom I do love ever,
      How can he leave me and go away far".

25

Rabindranath Tagore :The Death and the Deathless
....

Death does laugh aloud, but this never-dying love,
Depressed by ceaseless deaths, spreading all over
This endless Universe, with her saddened eyes
With steaming tears, with her anxious eagers,
In trembling heart, pulling every thing towards her.
          Hopelessly tired hopes,
     Laid down a curtain of fogs of sadness,
               Covering the Universe ! Thruth is that.

Hence, I hear a murmuring in the hearts of trees,
With eagerly anxious; With lethargic indifference
          Winds are playing with dead leaves,
               All meaningless games,
     In the hot air of this mid-day Autumn Sun.
               Days are dying out slowly,
Extending their shadows beneath the Baniyan tree.
          Heard an eternal flute,
     Seemingly playing a pastoral song
          Saddening valleys of the whole Universe .
The depressed Earth is sitting alone
               with her unbound hairs
On the bank of the Ganges,
          facing the wide fields of crops,
Putting up a thin cloth,
               made of golden-rays of mid-day sun
                    Covering her depressed chest.
Fixed are her eyes, within the deep blue sky,
 No words on her mouth .I recollect, then,
 I saw my daughter's pale face,
               seemingly the same,
Silently at door-step, with her
                    broken heart, As I told,
This Earth looks same like
               my daughter, four years old.

                    ****

                         26

8. Come back calls on my day of demise
[Aamar jaabar belay pihhu daake]

On my day of demise, who are they,
    Calling me to come back ?
Behold, there Morning Rays, calling me
    Through broken pieces of clouds;

The depressed birds
of rainy morning are chirping-
To call back me from the secret
branches of forest-trees !!

Swollen up the rivers, see, running so fast,
 Beneath the shadows of tree branches ,
 Closed to the banks on both sides,
Whom these rivers are searching for,
 Seems to give a call for backing come !!

Who is there from within me,
          again and again ,
Also sending a come-back call,
    In this depressed morning !
      ****

9.Deceiptive Complexity of Creation
   ### [Peace of mind by successful assimilation]
   [Tomaar sristir path rekhechho aakeerna kari]

The Passage of your creation, fully laid up
With the tricky nets of diverse deceptions;
Oh, the Nature, the Lady of secret tricks .
False assurance, entrapped by
                    your skillful hands
              In the lives of faithful ones.
You made this deceptive character, a colorable
                    hallmark of your greatness
There is no secret nightly-route[to unearth you].

But the roads are shown by
                    your stars and planets
The route to reach to the core
                    of creation's hearts,
That is eternally transparent,
                    by their faithful nature
That made themselves so eternally glitter .

Though looking complex from outside,
                    but internally transparent-
She is proud of that fact .
                    People feel themselves mocked
They are to meet the truth
Washed up their wisdom by the
                    own by the hearts.

Rabindranath Tagore :The Death and the Deathless
Nothing can totally deceive
            the inquisitive man .
He gets away with his final prize,
                        earned by own.

And stock that in chest of
            [knowledge and realization]
Whoever could absolve these
                    deceptions at ease,

He only gets from your hand
            The permanent rights to peace
[of mind, by successful assimilation
            of all the apparent contradictions].
                    ****

29

10. Unbroken Relation though spouse has died

At this end on Earth, the Groom lives on-
The bride has gone
In the other side of this living world.

There happens to be an invisible bridge
made up by them.
There pours down
The gift of the God;
The flute [of the Lord] plays
his tunes on that spot !!

Crossing the current of separation,
A ferry boat comes and goes on,
Takes them on the bank of
[mental [re-union.
The hearts of them ,   again and again
Shall keep crossing the river
to meet always and ever-
In the fields of happy conjugation.

At this side on Earth,
the groom sits at
Beneath the old Banyan tree,
The river goes on flowing in between,
The bride is seen
Then appearing; then
On the other side of that river,
Lover's flute goes on playing tunes-
always and ever..

****

11. Good-bye my darling, Good-bye
[kaler jatrar dvani shunite ki paao]

Can you hear the uproars of the passing time
It's chariot is in an eternally vanishing spirit
Raising the heart-throb of the entire sky,
Grinding the darkness by it's wheels,
Bursting the stars, crying to go into oblivion.

Alas my darling, that fleeting time
Grabbed me suddenly throwing his net
Put me on that flying chariot
On it's adventurous travelling path
Far, very far away from you !

It seemed to me, uncounted deaths,
 I came passing through-
Today at the pick-point of mountain,
                on a new dawn
The restless speeding force of the chariot
Even now flagging off my old name .

But still there is no way to return back;
Even you can see me from such a distance,
You won't be able to recognize me
            any more, here or there,
                Good bye , so my dear !!

If ever on some day, in work-less total leisure
In the fragrant breeze of a Spring,

Rabindranath Tagore :The Death and the Deathless

A mournful sigh shall flow in the nights,
 coming from the shore of a forgotten past,
When sobbing fallen Bakula sadden the sky,
Search out only at that time,
Something that I left behind for you,
The only thing that solely of mine-
At the deeper end of your soul,
in a forgetful evening,-
It might candle up a halo,
may even appear as
embodiment of a nameless dreams.

But that was never a dream
by any means .
To me that was my highest truth,
that is the deathless, sure,
It's my Love, that I have left behind
for you, oh dear,

That's my unchangeable offerings,
dedicated for ever,
Though I shall be going on and on ,
to unknow forward land ,
Flowing with the currents of change,
Along with flow of time; Hence,
here from I do convey from
The heat of mine,
My Good bye, my friend, last good bye .

****

32

CHAPTER-3
[Poems of painful memoirs & tombs]

12. TEARS OF STONES [SHAJAHAN/BALAKA-7TH POEM]

Shahajahan, the Lord of India, in the past
                    you knew all that-
The stream of time flashes away life,
                    riches and regards,
But only your pains of heart
Must breath eternally, that
                    was your imperial vows.
The Imperial powers look
                    as strong as thunders,
May die out in a drowsy dream
                    of reddish evening sky,
But his single sigh of long-breath
                    [of death-pain]
Must daily usurp up to sadden the sky
 all over, that was your desire of heart.
The heaps of diamonds,
                    pearls, gold and gems,
Like the magical rainbows of horizon's vacuum.
                    if vanishes one day, let that be-
But let only stay always and ever-
                    A single drop of her tears
Remain dazzling on the forehead
                                of time eternal
In the shape of this Tajmahal !
Time is flying out, it waits for none,
Oh, the Emperor, hence your anxious heart
Wanted to entrap the heart of floating time

Rabindranath Tagore :The Death and the Deathless
Binding with the alluring beauties,
Swinging on his neck a garland of décor
Giving him a grand receptions,
Offering an incredible form of beauty
        for representing a formless death.
Time does not permit to cry and shed tears
All through the months and years,
Hence you solidified your cries endless ,
Tying up tightly with the stones of silence ;

In the moonlit nights, in your private palatial bed
        To your beloved,
By her nick-name, used to call slowly her ears ,
That secret nick-name call,
                        you now planted here
            in the ears of eternity !
The extreme tenderly softness of love,
                Blossomed that-
In the flower-flashing beauty on silent marbles.

Oh, the Emperor, the poet,
It is, nothing but, the paintings of your heart
It is your fresh new Meghdut verses,
Unprecedented and wonderful
With rhythms and tunes,
Flying up towards the direction unseen
Where-ever your depressed beloved
Got now mingled up,
May be in the reddish rays of early dawns
May be in the moon-light, in the formless
fragrance of playful Chameli flowers,
On the shores beyond reaches of words,
The begging eyes often comes back there
            from that closed sphere.

But your ambassador of beauty, for ages,
Escaping the eyes of the guards of time,
Conveying your speechless message-

" I have not forgot, not forgot,
        Never forgotten you my beloved !!
            ****

13. A Mid-night Silent Departure

Mid-night then, left your home alone -
Never traveled before, road unknown.
While going, failed to say anything
None could say any farewell word,
World in slumbers, alone got out there
Searched in darkness, nowhere you were.

With love, day out and day in, for years,
The home you created by your own hands,
Fulfilling with accumulated affections
Today you left that, taking nothing back.

Only one question troubling in my mind, I see,
Oh, the wishful lady, why you went before me
Gone for laying by your tenderly hands ,
My sleeping bed for that eternal evening

****

****

14. Still do remember me

Still do remember me !!
   If   I go away a bit far,
        If under a slab of new love,
   our old one gets buried up,
        [Still do remember me] !

Even if I do stay near by,
   And you can't see me,
        like a faded shadow,
           that exists or not;
        Still do remember me !   2

If ever, some tears do appear,
           in your eyes,
   If in a night of Spring-breeze,
      Your pleasure plays flop,
   Or if in a Autumn morning,
You feel detested in working,
At that time , you remember me !

If by remembering me, there
Drops of tears no more appear,
        in the corner of your eyes,
        Still do remember me !!

****

15. REMEMBER THAT I SANG FOR YOU
[Ei katha ti mone rekho]

This much you must keep in mind,
That I joined in your plays and laughter
And that I sung some songs,
In those end-days [of my life]
 while old leaves do shed down.

Over the dry leaves in empty forest,
          in my own mind,
Disregarded and neglected,
             in an earth unkind;
I went on singing my songs,
 In those days when old leave sheds .

The day-travelers do remember,
                 I had to fight-
A I had been passing through my nights
Taking my night-lamp in my hand, so tough.

When got call from the other side the world afloat
I departed this shore rowing my broken boat.

   Till then I sung some songs,
     In those days when old leaves shed.

****

Link "https://youtu.be/4vurfNUc77E"
Sung by – Hemanta Mikhopadyaya

CHAPTER-4
[Silent Soliloquy with the beloved demised]

16.YOUR TOMB IS HERE, BUT WHERE ARE YOU
[Part of Sahjaahan, -BALAKA-7TH POEM]

Alas, the human hearts, again and again,
Can't look back to someone,
      No, No, there is no time;
You are flowing fast with fierce current of life,
From one port to the port of this world;
Load your cargo from one market place
Empty them fully in another port land .

By the murmuring of the Southern winds,
      In the gardens afresh,
The budding branches of Madhabi
      in the Spring time
When does cover up the restless scarf-ends of
Creepers, the farewell evening dusts bring
      all petals down to the Earth.
      Again time runs short-
Hence again in the dew-dropping nights
The gardens get filled up with new Kunda Flowers ,
to decorate the delighting strays by tear-filled
      flowers of Autumn months.

Rabindranath Tagore :The Death and the Deathless
Oh, the human hearts,

           all that you collected and saved
You have only to throw on road

                at the end of the day
and at the end of the night-

      No time, there no time, to stay and stop.

The tomb on the graveyard, stays at a place for ever;
Standing on the soil of the Earth,

           burying down the death
      Under covering cloths of memories;
Who can, but, bind up the flow of life.
Every star of the sky is calling up the life.

His invitation is from all the ends of horizon,
In the new lights over hills of rising suns.
Tearing the Knots of Memory-nets
He goes out running into the boundless

         expanse of this Universe.

Oh the King of the Kings,

         no kingdom could ever,

           Catch and arrest him ;
This ocean-fed Earth, could not fill you up,
Oh the Great ,Hence , you leave this Earth,
Enjoying the festival of life, you walk away,
kicking out by feet, this Earth,

        as if some used up potteries .

Rabindranath Tagore :The Death and the Deathless

You have gone far away
        But the seeds you planted here
Raising heads in the high sky
        Telling out in the resounding tunes -
"Whatever distance my sights
                can reach, ever-
    I do find that traveler no where.
                Around, nowhere."

His darling did not keep him,
        Kingdom opened his gate,
Not even prevented by Oceans and Mountains .

 Today his chariot, traveling by the
                        signals of nights
    Following the tunes of the stars
Towards the lion-gate of a new dawn,

Hence,
Under the weight of memories,
        I am stranded, and grounded down;
But the weightless he is no more here around .

****

40

17. **Formless you are within me**

No, no, you are not a portrait in frame,
Who says you are tied up
    by the lines and shed,
      along with your silent sobbing !!

Did I forget you ever any time .
You have made your nest inside
          the root of my life;
If I was ignorant of that,
          it is not a forgetfulness;
From backyard of that unmindfulness,
            you had been ,
Pulsating your messages
        through my blood and vein.

No more, you are, in front of my eyes,
As placed yourself within my eyes, by now ;
That's why [I do see you] greenish in the field,
Blue in sky , and in the whole world of mine,
You remain mingled so good so fine.

Did I ever know, does anybody know,
All these are your tunes,
      that only play in my songs ;
You are the real poet within this poet,
You are not, you are not,
           never only a portrait.
I got you, on a hay day of my life's morning -
And then lost you in the darkness of night .
 Now in these dark days again,
      unnoticed I found you in my within.
 You are no more a portrait,
          not a portrait, for mine.

18. Silently stay silently in My Heart

You live in the silent abode
                Of my heart-
Alone in solitude like a
                    full moon night.

My life my youthfulness and
                whole of mine,
You fill up with pride in silence,
                    like a night.

Your pitiful eyes shall only
                keep watch on me
You me covered with extended
                parts of your cloths.

My pains and pathos and
                my fulfilled dreams,
You fill up both with fragrance
                    as night does.

*****

19. Searching again my beloved's Gift

In case again I can, must shot
And search out that very cot !
On the lap of which, are laid down
The message of loving care,
Of that lady foreigner.

The fled away dreams of the past
Again be crowed there on, a must
In her unheard humming sound
Again a nest be created around.

The happy memories shall call back again,
And make the sleepless time sweeten
The Flute that has gone into silence
Shall bring back it's tune again thence.

At the window, her embracing open hands
Shall gaze at the roads of Spring's fragrance,
Footsteps of the entity, one that great soundless
Shall though be resonant in the deep dark space !

Oh, my Love from a distant land
Who laid this bed by her own hand,
The cot shall retain in it's ear ,
Retain my beloved's voices ever.

Her language I did not known really,
Only whose eyes spoke so eloquently.
This cot shall keep alive on and on
Sad tones of her message of separation

****

20. FILL UP THE JAR OF SEPARATION
WITH THE NECTAR OF SWEET MEMORIES
[Bhora Thak Smriti Sudhay]

Let the nectar of sweet memories
The jar of separetion ;
On the day of re-union
Bring that back !!

The tears of sad depression
Buried in the core of silence heart
Must secretly blossom up
As new expression of the heart.

You will be alone to cover the whole
passage of your journey,
There shall be darkness in your eyes,
But there shall be light in concentrated hopes.

The whole day, silently and secretly
The juice of nectar be poured down
upon your soul
Seating in lotus garden inside your heart,
From the tunes of strings of Lute of separation.

****

Link- https://youtu.be/II7NY4ixVrc
Sung by - Jayati Chakraborty

21.Pains of separation got sweetened today

Pains of separation sweetened today
In this springful night;
The tunes of deeper feelings,
Emerged out of deep passions.

Filled up the moonlit nights
The restless thirst of meetings
What a pitiable mirage emerges
Between the winks of my eyes .

Floating fragrance from distance
climbing on the shoulder of winds ,
Have been roaming inside my heart,
directionless.

It is these message, in which tunes and pitch,
Murmuring in the clusters of leaves,
Generating rythmns in my dancing rings
Spontenously !!

....

22. SHADOWS OF MY BELOVED FLASHES ON THE CLOUDS

Shadows of my beloved,
Now I can see floating in the sky, Alas,
Today, her saddening sighs,
Blow out of the rainy breeze...Alas !

My beloved peeps through the scattered clouds,
Hiding behind the evening star, to whom she looks.
Does the evening lamp's put out flames,
Comes now to her remembrance !!

Taking the fragrance of the rain-drenched forests,
My beloved makes the garlands not for touches ;
Within ceaseless pours of the condensed rainy cloud,
 My beloved lost her words of heart in sky, wide out.

The garments of my beloved,
seen flapping over the dense forest,
Blown up by the excited breaths of
the greenish groves so unrest .

....
Link= https://youtu.be/EONsYl3sYes
Sung by- Hemanta Mikhopadhyaya

....

CHAPTER-4

[Nothing is Lost in Thy Universe- as all are sheltered at thy feet]

23. So little possess, heart breaks, if anything I loss

[Alpo loyaa thaaki taai mor jaaha jaay taaha jaay]

Whatever little I have, hence from that-
Whatever goes, is a great loss that do hurt.
May it be an atom or it's particle,
My soul does cry and wail.

The river-beds and banks, try to uselessly,
To prevent or hold back water floating forcibly.
Thus only, blowing the knocks on the heart,
The waves and currents flee away apart.

Whatever goes away and whatever remains
If I give out to you for safe keepings,
There nothing is lost, everything survive
In thy great grace, in thy Universe so alive.

In thy creation, stars and planets endless,
None is lost, not even atom and articles.
Why then not my small articles, indeed-
Shall not remain safe at thy feet.

****

- LINK "https://youtu.be/Ka1IyXNdUL4"4
Sung by – Susmita Patra,

....

24. Death pains, take solace at his feet

There are pains, there are deaths,
Heart burns with flares of separation-
Still you feel the end-peace
The ultimate ecstasy of pleasure,
Still the Universe is flowing all over.

Still the flow of life is a continuous,
The Sun, the moon and the stars
Throw some smiles to us,
Springs comes to gardens,
Affectionally and so wonderous.

Flowers drop down, new flower blooms,
Waves wipe out, new waves emerge-
There is final demise, no final end,
There is no smallest vacuum
in the space,
Do find peace of mind,
Surrendering at His feet,
Who is the One,
always full and complete.

****

25.In Thy Universe , Nothing is Lost

[ENERGY AND FORMS INTER-CHANGE,
KEEPING THE AGGREGATE EQUAL]

In thy endless expanse [of space]
Whatever I road at whatever distance,
There is nothing called sorrows or death,
Not even a sign of separation-
In thy endless expanse
I travel at whatever distance...[1]

Death appears as a death,
Sorrows appears as a dug-well full of pains ,
When forgetting to gaze towards you,
I do only look into myself......[2]

At thy feet, oh, the ONE with who is ever
full and total,
Whatever exists, exist here,
The fear of losing is only lying within me,
And that is why , days and night, I cry..[3]

The fatigues of the heart, the strains of livelihood,
Within a wink of my eyelid, instantly they vanish
When I can visualize your true reality in life
And keep that within me. [4]
****

Link- "https://youtu.be/MeVJp8F75Gw"Gw
Sung by- Piya Chakraborty;
Link- https://youtu.be/6ag2NgNl82g
Sung by- Jayati Chakraborty

49

26. Oh, the helmsman of my life-boat,]

Oh, the helmsman of my life-boat,
Where do you park my boat ,
During low-tide period on our deaths
The blue sky through it's grand silence
Brings the celescele message from end distance
The days do pass on singing aimless songs
On the unknown endless vacuum
Oh, the helmsman of my life-boat,
My blood is stringing by the tunes
Of your mysterious hymns
Nights are vibrant with the
Blows of Conch in deep sounds.

The endless time flowing alone
Singing songs of unending separation
The vacuum sky helps to spreads on
The covering net of sad depression
You the great helmsman of my life-game
Going on great generating bubbles of stars' clusters
All over the wide expanse of the Ganges of sky

When drum of death plays within your chest
Neither speedily nor causing delays
The lines between of life's and death's boundary lines
Amalgamate in subtle precision ,
You then sail my boat of life
For my last journey, reveal to me, my Helmsman
All about that unconceivable non-dark land,
Covered by endless darkness of our total ignorance.
****

27. In the blissful land of auspicious light-

In Thy blissful land   of auspicious light
I saw Thou flashing ,
In the form of Truth and Beauty.
Thy divine grace   ever manifested
In the endless space,
The Galaxies are   thy glittering gems
Around your dancing feet.

The stars and planets   the Suns and moons
Eagerly in a race,
Drinking up   and taking baths
In thy unending rays.
On this Earth   Dances down the streams
Alluring sweet faces of beauties,
Flowers and leaves   tunes and fragrance
Enchanting are the colors;

Flowing the lives,   days and nights
Eternally afresh stream,
It's thy kindness   always ceaseless
In the births and deaths always.
Affection and love   kindness and devotion
Softens our souls,
Endless solaces   pouring downs on us
To reduce our burns.

.

The Universe is thy   festive ground
Creation praises you.
Wealth of goodness   Knowledge endless
And fearlessness lies in thy feet.

PART-II
[Towards Realization of Death-less-ness]
CHAPTER -5
[Solace-Syten-1 : Accepting Death- as an Act of God]

28. Why show thy terrific face, my Lord

Why is thus thy Devastating face,
with red-eyes sparking in the dark-clouds,
Smashing the chest of the evening sky,
By thy arrows of thundering and lightening.

Oh, the embodiment of beauty and bliss,
 the flowers were eagerly waited on the branches,
 but by thy storming knocks,
        they fell and mingled in the dust.

Why in this spring time,
meant for enchanting the beings,
     Thou hast hidden thy graceful
              face of sweetness?
Why frighten the frightened,
         art these thy cruel games?
If by this heavy blow, wish to tear our bonds
         with these mortal lives,
Forcibly collecting us to put into boxes
for permanent rest and liberation

****

29. No no no , you dot not play
a joyful game always

No no no , you don't play a joyful game always,
        Between you and me, the game
              was never the same,
In my whole life, during nights and the days.
It was never a very pleasant play always.

Many a time, the candle-lights extinguished,
The nightly Cyclone came howling and roaring,
        The cradle of the life [on Earth]
    Received suspicious back-pushes, un-worth.

Repeatedly broking dams and bridges,
Did the flood water -all the damages,
In those hard days, wailings filled all sides.
Oh, the rudely mighty, in sorrows and happiness,
This message is striking my heart-

    In thy love, there might be hammerings,
But there is no careless indifferences to the beings.
           ****

 LINK "https://youtu.be/vbitFJ0_-I8"8
Sung by Babul Supriyo & Alaka Yagnik

30. Why emptied my house in mid-night, my Lord [Aji bijana ghare nishita rate..ashbe jadi]

To-day in my deserted house,
                    in this mid-night,
  you came with your empty hands,
I am never afraid of that sad situations,
I know, my friend, I surely believe,
You have your hands behind all these.

Days are spent out somehow,
Only on the passage of desires and acquisitions,
Now time has come,
to bring me before you and surrender
Let the darkness stay covering the sky- truly blinded,
But let thy [sparkling] touch fill my heart,
                    and keep lighted.

Swinging on the cradles of life,
    Forgot the life's value itself,
Now the swinging between life and death,
May you please to take me where you wish.
****
LINK "https://youtu.be/nTWpFP4IQNM"
Sung by-Rezwana Choudhry Banya
      LINK "https://youtu.be/jkcDydsPr0I"I =
Sung by- Hemanta Mukhopadhy

31. To win over sufferings, you are to go through it [Dukha jadi naa paabe to dukkha tomaar]

Without going through sufferings,
How can your sufferings end ever ?
Poison has to be burnt to death
   By the burning power of poison .

Allow your fire to rise up in flame
      Never fear the fire,
When it will die out into ashes
It's burning power entirely vanishes.

Never try to fly and hide
   Face it going straight ,
Running to avoid , through a long race
  You only prolong your distress .
Dying again and again,
Make the death die for ever,

Then only that life will come,
And himself take his seat of own .

. . . .

32. Thy propitious lights emerges
out of the darkness of sorrows
[Dukhr timire jadi jwale tabo mangala-alok]

Out of the darkness of
      pains and sorrows-
If thy propitious lights emerge,
      Then, let that so happens.

If death takes us to thy
      land of deathlessness,
Let then that happens.

If the flame of my burning
      candle in worship hall,
Burns down also my heart-burm
Let then do that happen.

If on my tear-filled eyes,
      draws the attention of
Thy affectionate eyes,
      Let then do that happen.

****

https://youtu.be/_5fUtWkkHbs
Sung- Sagar Sen & Indrani Sen

33.He desires we live, He desires we die

He desires so we live, He desires so we die.
Say all praises only for Him .
God is a grace in this world,
By his grace rulers rule,
We see His grace in the graveyards,
God is great, God is great !

When he maddens us pleasure of nectar, is great !
When he makes us to cry on Earth, he is great !
On the lapsand breasts of our nears and deas
We we see his smiling face, He is great ,
When he burns down our happy houses,
                              it is His grace
All praises go to the Almighty , the great.

When He himself comes to us in smilingly,
                    it is his grace
When he makes us roaming in countries for shelter,
                    he is always great.

He is great in Land and waters,
He is great in fruits and flowers
He is great when he stands on the lotus of our heart,
Blissfully delighting by beaming hollows of your feet
God , you are graceful, you are graceful.

****

34. Fight the dreadful, He is with you
[Prachanda Garjane Ashilo eki durdin]

What a sorrowful time appeared
                    with bursting furors -
Crowded clouds, thunders are
                sending ceaseless threats.

Nights are bitten by the snakes
                   of frequents lightnings,
In this darkness, sky is shedding
                tears with loud cryings.

Daring the dreads, raise up those,
                    fearful and idle,
Generate inner powers, pleasantly
                   in your hearts.

Open up fearless eyes,
                see the incredible scene,
Seated upon the throne of the
                grandest threats,
The One who shatters the dangers
                and remove the fear
And see the tranquility got
                restored every where.

****

35. I shall cross the sea of death
[Aami marer sagar paari dibo bhisan jharer baaye]

I shall cross the sea of death
Sailing against the fierce winds of tempest,
Using this fear-tearing boat of mine .

With full faiths in "never-fear"-doctrine
Fixing my torn up sail, with my boosting heart,
I shall surely reach to your other shore,
And anchor beneath the shadowing Banyan Tree.

He will show me the right route who wants me here,
To sail my boat with fearless heart
Is the only responsibility left out to me .

When the day will end ,I know for sure,
I shall reach to your shore,
And offer the red lotus of my bloody sufferings,
At Thy emotive   feet .
                    ****

LINK "https://youtu.be/4oPlsztJo0s"s
          Sung by- Piyush Kanti Sarkar
                  ....

36. Empower me, my Lord, to fight out my odds.
   [Bipade more Raksha karo -e nohe mor prarthanaa]]

Save me in my danger- that is not my prayer
See that to face danger, I do never fear.
In my pains and sufferings,
Solace is not I am expecting
See that I can win over the
sufferings always and ever.

If I don't get any help at all,
 My might shall never fall
By losses in earthly matters,
by deceptions from near and dears
My mind must not suffer the decadence.

You should rescue me, That is not my prayer
See that I have power to be my own saver.
By making my burdens less,
 no need to give me solace
See that I can carry my burdens ever.

With bent up head, in my happy days-
        I must trace your face,
If everyone in this Earth, in my distressed night,
deceive me, deprive and fight,
See that I never develop any doubts in you.
                    ****

37. Stage Play of Death [Poem No.14 of Shesh-Lekha]

The dark nights of sufferings, again and again,
Appeared before my house-door and came in,
Only weapon I saw in his possession
The perverted scenes of pains, dangerous poses
                    of a terrifying play
These are all his deceptive game-play in the dark.
Those many times, got away with his masks of fears
That many times I suffered defeats
                    and losses for no reason.

These games of loss and gains,
            are useless illusions of life;
These tied up horrors dragging our legs
            from the very childhood;
Are just acts of satires made on
            our false fear of pains.
The movie films of diverse acts of fears
Is the skillful Art of Death,
            Painted on the widened
            canvas of darkness.

....

****

38. LIOANS OF DEATHS ROARING AROUND [BALAKA- POEM NO.17]

Are you listening the roars of Deaths,
from a safe distance,
Oh the poor heart,
shame to your indifference !

The clamor of mournful crying, apart-
The Gussying out streams of blood
from millions of bursting hearts!
The mighty waves of flooding flames,
The stormy clouds of poisonous rains,

On the surface of Earth down
and Sky upward,
Fainted, exhausted, they are falling forward
for embracing the daring deaths ;
Now, navigating through that ghastly
streams,
Sailing down the Seas,
Need is there to lead the vessel
to a new safe shore.
The Captain's call
And his command has come after all,
'Time is up for good to tear
the tie with his port,
Age-old trading with your saved currencies,
any more
Shall not work here in this port and shore .
Cropped in are the deceptions,

　Goodwill capital of truthfulness are gone'

　　　　Hence our Captain calls
　" Despite tempest, we must sail
　　And take the vessel at a new shore ."

Forthwith came sailors leaving home, afore.
　Gathered from all corners,
　　　　taking in hands their ores,
　Suddenly getting up from deep slumbers.
The condensed clouds of tempest over,
　　　Darkened the sky; Sailors do not know-
　　　How much of night is still to go ;

　Horizons are filled with foams of waves,
　　Still then, the Captain, calls and urges-
　　　" The vessel must start afore,
　　　　and must reach to some new shore".

　Came out the braves without fears,
　Mothers came crying behind, with tears,
The wives were wiping,
　　　　　standing at the door gates.
　Within that roaring and howling tempest,
　Cries of separation sounded atop non-rest.

　　　Beds of comforts ended for
　　　　the Householders,
　"Sail and proceed, sail and proceed, the
　　　　voyagers"

　　Came the commanding order,

" Time of trading in this port is over ".
Sounded also in the roars of tempest high-
Frightening invitations,
came from the voids of sky.
The songs of deaths, re-sounded
over and always-
Sailors moved on, for a new life,
in a dreamful voyage,
In the seas, engulfed by the
deepened darkness .

All the sorrows of this Earth, all sins,
all adversities
All the tears, all hatred, and animosities.
Have raised up in high waves
of time all arounds,
To flood over the shores,
And banks, all that bounds.
Still to proceed, rowing the vessel away,
Got to cross all odds on the way;

With ears filled with bursting cries of
civilization
With head-load of threatening insane
devastation.
Still with endless hopes in heart,
moved on their ores

The fearless braves,
suppressing all the sorrows.

Oh, my brother, whom do you blame,
                    what it means,
Bow down your head,
            these are results of all our sins.
These sins, committed by all of us,
                    what a pity-
Generated these angers
                    in the heart of the Almighty,
            Ages of faults accumulated in
            North West End*-

The cowardice acts of coward, that owns-
The desperate crimes of the mighty ones.
        The grave greed of the greedy,
                    brews and howls
        As the eternal discontents of the
                    deprived souls.

        The prides of castes, creeds and races,
                    with certainty
        Caused Countless insulation
                    to goddess of Humanity
Now the broken tolerance of the Gods,
        Roaming around in lands and waters,
            Now that this severe sighs
            in the form of Cyclones,

Fell on Earth and seas,
                    with   stubborn tones -
Let all extinguish, all fires of
                    the thundering arrows

65

Clean up all sins from
this unhappy world always-

Stop blaming, stop your claims
of false holiness,
Just with single object in hearts of
all and one,
Cross this Sea of devastation,
Reach to the shore of new creation,
To raise heads and hand,
On your new built victory stand !!

[now addressing the God ....]

Diving into the heart of deaths,
If nectars of life never enter in their
bread and breaths,
Truth is not established fighting
with the sorrows,
Sins do not die out of its
shame of own existence,
Egotism not crushed under
heaviness excess decors

Then, why these left-home
heroes were sent apart,
Given the assured voice
in their faithful heart,

Rabindranath Tagore :The Death and the Deathless

Why jumped to deaths, in hundreds
and thousands,
Just like that, millions of stars
went into oblivions ?

With false faiths to see rise of some
delightful dawns ?
The flooded bloods of the braves,
The floating tears the mothers' eyes,
Can price of these valueless offerings,
Shall bite the dusts of this Earth
rugged and raven,
The price is still be enough
to buy the heaven ?

Shall not the treasurer of this Universe,
Pay out His debts, as a declared insolvent thus?
Shall not a rightful of devoted service,
Bring a day full of delights.

In the fierce nights of terrible sufferings,
Testing the blows of the deaths,
When the humans crossed
all earthly limits, then
Shall not the divine grace of
God, resurrect again ?
....
* the direction wherefrom devastating Winds hit India

****

39. To win over sufferings
you are to go through it

[Dukha jadi naa pabi to dikha tomaar ghuchbe kabe]

Without going through sufferings
     How can your sufferings ever end ?
Poison has to be burnt to death
       By the burning power of poison .

Allow your fire to rise up in flame
         Never fear the fire,
When it will die out into ashes
     It's burning power entirely vanishes.

Never try to fly and hide
        Face it going straight ,
Running to avoid , through a long race
      You only prolong your distress .

Dying again and again,
      Make the death die for ever;
Then only that life will come,
      And himself take the seat of his own .
          ****

Link- https://youtu.be/2iws3KKqlxw
  Sung by- Sumitra Sen

40. Let come Victory, Let come new Dawn
[Joy hok, Joy hok, Nabo Arunodaya]

Let come victory, let come new dawn,
Be the eastern sky-glittered by the Sun....

Let come undefeated wisdom,
Destroying the dogma's kingdom,
Let fears and feebleness be gone,
Let us get free from apprehension 2

Let Come undying hopes,
Let inertia, lethargy goes;

Let the crying and sobbing eliminated,
And Bonded get emancipated.
****

LINK "https://youtu.be/-k3U8FbKikM"FbKikM
Sung – Pijushkanti Sarkar;
Extra= VIDEO -LINK
"https://youtu.be/m9R5yzHkYUc"yzHkYUc
Sung by-Celebration of Rabindra-Nazrul Jayanti -2016
-by Tagore Society of Houston, Texas
Sung by- Sushmita Patra

****

41. NO FEAR , VICTORY MUST COME
[Naai naai bhoy, habe habe joy]

Fear Not, For thou shalt conquer,
Thy doors will open, thy bonds break
Often thou losest thyself in sleep,
And yet must find back thy world ,
Again and again.

The call comes to thee from the earth and sky
The call from among men,
The call to sing of gladness and pain,
Of shame and fear.

The leaves and the flowers,
The waters that fall and flow,
Ask for thy notes to mingle with their own,

The darkness and light
To tremble in the rhythm of thy song.
****

Translated by- Rabindranath Tagore himself
****

Link -https://youtu.be/-k3U8FbKikM
Sung by- Pijush Kanti Sarkar
****

CHAPERT-8 :
Now Loosen your earthly bonds.

42. Let these songs tea off your ties

The melodious tunes shall be melting down
All your chains and bonds with your own.
In the darkness of arrested thoughts and voice
Your soul shall cry, if made remain expression-less.1

In the heart of poet of this Universe,
        Wherefrom musical heptachord sonds
Let your life, take a deep dive
--------------------into that stream of tunes!

Lost of tunes and rhythms,
        soul suffers confusion, though fake,
Within inner you and outer you,
                symphonies break.

The life, Lost of tunes, is an impediment,
   a darkness and obstacle,
Tune your life with the divine tunes
   and get rid of the riddle.

Rabindranath Tagore :The Death and the Deathless
****

43.. Uplift me from my fears to
Thy fearlessness

[Bhoy hote tabo aboy majhare- natun janam]
****

From fear to fearlessness, My Lord,
Give me a re-birth.
From emptiness to the eternal riches,
From doubtfulness to temple of Truth,
From inertia to new liveliness,
Give me a birth afresh.

From my own desires, My Lord,
Put me into what you desired,
From my selfish acts-
To thy propitious tasks
From the many, to thy Oneness,
From pleasures and pains to the lap of the peace
From myself, into thyself,
Give me a new life, my Lord !
****

LINK- "https://youtu.be/a7XcOCx7XMc"XMc
Sung by = Corus =Direction : Sumitra Chatterjee
....

44. Why suffer so much of apprehension- to step out of that door
[kenore ei duyaar tuku paar hote sangsay]

Why so much suspicious about,
                to pass out through that door ?
        Say victorious welcome to the Unknown!

On this side you have all the faith,
            for that side you are afraid ;
Say victorious welcome to the Unknown!

In your known household,
        spent days with tears and laughter;
For travelling to the other corner,
            your mind is ready ever =
Say victorious welcome to the Unknown!

You have made the death an alien, my dear,
Thus you made you life insignificant for ever.
If your household bounded by days,
            can accommodate all and one,
Then can your eternal place of stay,
            be a land of total vacuum.
Say victorious welcome to the Unknown!

****

Link-https://youtu.be/su9_dulspSY
Sung by- Suchitra Mitra

Rabindranath Tagore :The Death and the Deathless

45. What is destined to be lost, why die to hold on that

[Jaa hariye jaay ta aagle rekhe, raibo kato aar]

That is perishable and lost,
Why to that closed in your chest,
How long shall you sit with that-
Spending sleepless night, I can't afford.
For that, Oh, my Lord.
No time even to think over that.

Living days and nights, Closing all the doors,
Whoever whatever, tends to enter,
Under suspicion of mine,
I drive them out, again and again,

That is how none can reach me
In my lonely home, [you see]
Your delightful world plays
Out of my closed room, beyond my eyes.

I seems, any path, you also did not get..
Came and went back, repeatedly, from my gate.
Whatever I retained, I have simply lost;
What I kept abreast, has done into the dust.

****

LINK - "https://youtu.be/o85UqCGl16c"c"
Sung by - – Rezwana Chodhury Banya

46. Who is that ferryman crossing river of death [Tumi epaar opaar karo ke go ogo kheyar neye]

Who   are ferrying men   from this   shore that
shore crossing [river of death]
Who are you the ferryman, as I have seen.
Sitting at my door, I gazing at that scene.

When village market is closed
Everyone returns back to their homes
To join my return trip, my dream roams.

In the evenings, you ferry sails forward
To take your boat to the other world.
Seeing that my mind becomes restless
The farewell songs comes out, effortless.

Seeing clamor of the dark water,
My eyes becomes effusive ever-
The golden beams coming from the other world
 Enchants my heart so much beyond any word.
There is no word in your mouth as I find
Oh, the ferryman, so no way to read your mind.
Whatever anything is indicated in your eyes

Oh, the ferryman, noticing you to guess .
If at any moment, on my face ,
Your eyes send a message with a stare ,
Then, my mind always says-
I must run to board your boat then and there.
 Oh , the ferryman on boat, yet,
[I am looking for that date]

CHAPTER-9
[Faith in Re-birth]

47.If you won't give my life back, how can you kill me

If you won't give my life back,
    How can you kill me then?
So much of clamor, then what for,
Throughout your this diverse creation.

Arrows of fire are piled in your stocking,
By your angry footsteps, Earth is trembling.
The life-giver, is seen involved in
His festive game of human killing.

My heart is so much broken and shattered.
 If the cause is not ever disclosed,
 Then whole thing appears so awkward.

Digging up the mines of our pains
You gathered the gems of your crowns.
May these crying of our deaths-
Pacify the Life-giver's unknown wraths.
    ****
Link-"https://youtu.be/2CKB_I3P6kU"kU
Sung by -Kanika Bandopadhyaya

48. I shall be back to the Earth Again
[Jakhan parbe na more payer chinna ei bate]

When my footprints not be seen on the dust of the Earth,
I shall no more row my ferryboat in this route,
And shall close down my trading of buying and selling
 Closing my ledger book of my receivables and debts,
My visits to these marketplaces shall come to an end.
May it be so that even you forget me then forever,
Gazing at the stars, never tried to locate me there !!

When may dust layer up on the strings of my Tanpura,
The thorn-thick bushes and creepers close my door-gates
May that my flower garden be covered up by thick grass,
As if the dressed up like those banished into forest land.
Moss might cover up embankments of my pond.
May it be then, you will forget me to remember,
Gazing at the stars, try not to locate me there   !!

Then also flutes will play tunes in the sky,
Days and nights will roll on ever,
Time will pass as it is passing on today,
From port to port, many more trading boats,
Shall be crowding here, and shall float .
Cattles be rearing in the grassland, shepherds will play,
May it be by then, you shall forget me forever-
Gazing at the stars, never tried to locate me there!!

Who says in that morning I shall be no where ?
I shall also be playing my games somewhere.
Only that, I shall be called by a new name,
Some new hands will drag on my shoulders
Thus shall I travel ever, the eternal me.
May it be then, you shall forget me forever-
May it be then, you no more search me in the stars.

77

49. If I fail to get you in this life-
I must remember till next life

If I fail to meet you my Lord
In this life, this time also, if I fail to accord,
Then that fact that I failed to meet ever,
Must remain in my memories in next life there.
Please see that, I do not forget that,
Even in my sleep and dreams,
And the fact of failure, must pain my heart,

In this Earth's marketplace-
As much as I spent my days ,
Though my hands got filled with fortune,
I really got nothing, that brings me with you in tune
May please be seen that I do not forget that fact -
And in my sleep and dreams- pains come to my heart.

If in my idle times, seating on my roadside path,
If on the dusty road, I lay my bed for rest at that,
As if whole length of road is still uncovered
That feel should come to my heart,
I do forget not, I must scream-
with all the pains , in my sleep and dream.

Even if when I burst in a laughter- ,
Or play my flute in my home ever,
Even if, my house, I intently décor -
I must remember, I failed to bring you home at ,
My mind must keep that fact intact.
See that I forget not,
In my sleep and dreams, that must pain my heart.

50.Now you take me to you, my Lord
[TUMI EBAR AAMAY LAHO]

Now you take me to you, my Lord
This time don't refuse me, Lord
Do grab and drag my heart to you .

My days gone without your touch
I don't like to look back at that,
Let those be buried into dust.
Now opening my life under your lights,
Let me always remain awakened.

In what illusion, by whose advise
I roamed around here and there
On roads and in the valleys,
Now I keep my ears near to you chest
Tell me your own messages.

Whatever guilt whatever deceptions
Might still be hidden
In the secret caves of my heart
No more for those you refuse me , Lord
Your fires must burn them to ashes .
****

Link- "https://youtu.be/nXbE7a8YPPs"YPPs
Sung by- Kanika Bandopadhya

51. Thou hast made me endless,
such is thy pleasure

[Aamare tumi je ashesh karechho, emoni leelaa abo]

[NB:-Tagore's own translation]

"Thou hast made me endless,
such is thy pleasure.
This frail vessel thou emptiest
again and again,
and fillest it ever with fresh life.

This little flute of a reed thou hast
carried over hills and dales, and hast
breathed through it melodies eternally new.

At the immortal touch of thy hands
my little heart loses its limits in joy and
gives birth to utterance ineffable.

Thy infinite gifts come to me
only on these very small hands of mine.
Ages pass, and still thou pourest,
and still there is room to fill."

NB:-FIRST POEM OF GEETANJALI -
****

CHAPTER-10
[FAITH IN LIBERATION]
[From whirling Cycle of births and deaths]

52. Let my coverage goes, liberation comes.

This my cover of darkness shall fade out,
 My body and mind will dip into eternal bliss. ১

From my eyes, the illusions will disappear,
The Universe will blossom in my heart as a Lotus,
In my life, Thy victory will be sounded. ২

My blood shall dance in the tune of the Universe,
My heart shall expand into the great grandeurs of life.

My heart shall vibrate in the tunes of lyre of light ,
Swing with the necklace of your stars;
My selfish desire shall go into oblivion. ৩

*****
LINK-https://youtu.be/jDtQ9A-4y8s"
Sung by Swagatalakshi Dasgupta

****

53. Have you enwrapped your own-self
[Apanare diye rachilire ki e aapanar e aabaran]

Is it that you have enwrapped you
        within your self ?
Open up door, you may find your
Abode of delight and pleasure.

Can't find liberation, outside anywhere
Even the sky has limitation like a prison
Breathing your enclosed air, hence like poison.

Open the barriers, light will come in
Throw out your self wide away,
Then only, your life easily;
Be filled in with nectar.

Keep your flute open and free
Let it be played by Him who is to play,
Beg nothing, that will ensure
Your feel, fulfilled with riches.

****

Link- https://youtu.be/TSp6zULEF64
Sung by – Kanika Banadhyopadhyay
………………………
Link- https://youtu.be/ddJbxYlDj_A
Sung by- Rezwana Choudhury

****

54. Take this for granted-
Liberation must be attained
[Ei kathaata dharei raakhis mukti toke]

Take this for granted,
You must get your liberation.
The passage that reaches
To the desired shore.

With fearless mind, in loud voice
Singing songs you will sail across
Happily, face the waves of tempest
You are to pass through the turbulence.

If circular currents rotate your boat
Save your vessel from that
On the road of journey, there must be thrones
Must you smash them to go forward.

To protect your happiness gabbing at the chest
Do not kill you in constant fears,
To live a life with fulfillment
You have got to taste some hammers of death .

      & &&&&&&&&&&&

Link- ht "https://youtu.be/CSpWh1Oy0ps"   Sung by- Arundhuti

******

55. I get my liberation in the sky, in it's light in the grass

I seek and I find my liberation in the sky,
In the lights of the celestial bodies,
In the grassland of this Earth.

I often do not find me, inside my body of mind,
I fly in the upper sky along
with the tunes of my songs,
And enjoy my liberty and liberation,
accomplished fully.

I find my liberation in the minds of mankind,
I find liberation in the hard tasks of public cause,
If it requires to dare to face sufferings and dangers.

In this festive ground of the supreme Creator,
In the fire-flaring altar of self-sacrifice,
I wish I could offer myself, to get my liberation.
Full and final, happy and total, and supreme one !

*****

****

56. Man only traversed into Universe to find you
[Mahabiswe Mahakaashe Mahakaal majhe]

In this great Universe,
Filling the great sky,
during the great span of time,
I am so alone, singularly travelling,
wonder-dumbed.

You being the Lord of the Universe,
Staying within your endless secrets of creation.
Soundlessly alone, staying within
Thy great abode of divine grace.

In this endless time and space,
In countless spheres of creations,
You are keeping your eyes on me,
I am also staying on always gazing at you.

Silent are here all the uproars,
Fathomless peace all over,
You are only ONE, and within Thee,
Me alone,[with your favor] living here
Without any fear.3
****
Linkhttps://youtu.be/MBB0PrE3mlU
Sung by- Abhik Deb

****

85

57. Endeavor to tear off the ties

[Bandhan Chedar sadhan habe ma-boirabe]

Endeavor to tear off the ties
        now or never -
I shall leave this shore-singing
        tunes "no-fear"

The victory garland,
is at someone's hand,
Holding burning flames
      of deadly fire
But Still I salute that
      devastating power.

Through the oceanic sky of time,
        light travels,
Nights and days, the cross
         to endless-space.

A wave of that sky-travel has sent me a call
Let the sounds of thunder
      throb my heart,
Proceed I must to mingle in
 festive of life there at.
    ****

Link -https://youtu.be/sdGUr-Vl7DQ
Sung By- Suchitra Sen
      ****

58. Ocean of tranquil peace is just in front.

[Samukhe Shanti Paarabar
bhasao tarani he karnadhar]]

An ocean of tranquil peace ,
In front, [be seen please] .
Sail my boat, thou my Boat's helm of affair, .
Thou shall be my eternal sailor ,
Take me , take me , on thy lap's [shelter].
On this road of infinitive journey [ever]
The eternal lighthouse shall the Northern Star .

Oh liberator,
thy forgiveness and kindness
Be my eternal sustenance
in this journey to endless .

Let this severe all my ties –
whatever be that earthly,
Let this big Universe-embrace and
put me on some valley;

May I thus starts up with a
fearless introduction
To thy great unknown Creation .

****

CHAPTER-11
[To meet and mingle with the Creator]

From "Sufi Concept to " Sohang-tattva" [I am He]
[Worshippers of Love with Lordship-status]
[Solace-system- 7th level- the highest level]

59. Beyond the boundaries of Life and Death, Thou standeth [Jeevan maraner seemaanaa chaaraye, rayechho daraye]]

Beyond the boundaries of Life and Death,
   I find thou, my friend, always standeth.

In the sky of my deserted heart, your great throne,
   seen covered down the lights.
With deepened hope, with condensed delight,
   I am gazing at you, opening my arms wide.

The silent night, washing your feet,
Has laid up her black hairs on the sky-path and street.

To-day, what a tune thus,
resounding in the universe,
Merging out of your Veena
[Veena-strings as such].

World is resounded with that tune's vibrance-
Within it's paining appeal-
I loss my exitence.
****

Sung by-Hemanta Mukhapadhyay

60. You started your journey
to meet me very long ago

You started your journey
        to meet me, ages gone away;
The Sun and the Moon
Have no power to block your way.

How many ages, days after days,
 I am getting the sounds your foot-steps,
 From your messengers,
        getting secret messages,
Direct into my heart always !!

Oh, the traveler, to-day flooding
           my soul wholly,
The waves of pleasure are
        throbbing restlessly !!

I have kept me ready leaving all works,
Winds are blowing up the fragrance,
Conveying signals of
your arrival with grace.

    ****

Rabindranath Tagore :The Death and the Deathless

61. I started my journey singing your songs in unknown past [kabe aami baahi holem]

When did I start my journey, singing your names,
On some unknown past-not on a date very nearby.
Forgotten the date when I started seeking you
Since some unknown past-not on a date very nearby.

As a spring comes down, not knowing, where it is going,
Similarly I floated down along with the flow of creation;
Since some unknown past-not on a date very nearby.

In many names I called you, painted different images,
In my own pleasure, ran hither and thither,
 not finding your right abode, any where ;
Since some unknown past-not on a date very nearby.

As flowers waits whole night,
         to get the morning light
Similarly my hopes to meet
                 you are heaped in my heart ,
Since some unknown past-not
                 on a date very nearby.

****

90

62. You have love for us, hence you love to meet us
[Taai tomaar aananda aamar pare,
tumi taai eshechho neeche]]

It is Thy pleasure that you find in me,
So, my lord, you came down to my door,
If I were not here, Oh, lord of the Universe,
Your love could be futile,
by not finding any place to fall upon thus.

With me you arranged this festive fare,
Through my heart your pleasure games plays,
Through my life-span your diverse desires
Have been flowing in waves after waves.

That's why being the Supreme Lord,
Still only to attract my heart-
Appearing in so many enchanting forms
Constantly alive in new creations.

Thence, my Lord, you came down here,
To spread your love in the hearts of the devotees
Your image mingled with my face
Completes your full manifestation.
....

63.That You and me shall have a conjugation
[Tomay aamay milan habe bole aaloy Aakash bharaa]

As, between you and me, there be a conjugal meet-
Hence the whole space has been filled with light,
As, between you and me, there be a conjugal meet-
This greenish Earth is flooded with flowers-so sweet .

As, between you and me, there be a conjugal meet-
The Universe is lying awaken on the lap of sky,
                              All through the night.
The goddess of the beaming dawns is coming daily,
                    to open the Eastern Gate ,
With clamor of chirps of the birds [and she does wait] .

The boat-of-hope for this final meet has been floating on
Through the river of time, from it's beginning unknown .
The flowers and buds, all through this unknown age,
Had been over-flooding the
                    reception-tray for this marriage!

As, between you and me,
                there has to be a final conjugation ,
On the festive platform of this universe,
                    ages are passing on.
My soul have been tracing out the route of your passage
Dressed up as a bride,
                eternally committed for this marriage !

                ****

64. Just I happened to conjugate with you
[Ei labhinu sanga tabo sundaro he sundaro]

It just happened that I could conjugate with you,
      Oh my Lord, the beautiful !
My body became purified and pious,
      Happily blessed became my soul;
Oh, my beloved, the beautiful, so beautiful !

New lights emerged out of my amused eyes
And they blossomed with new sights;
The sky of my heart got thickly filled in
By the fragrant breeze, generated within.

By your sweet touches, my heart
      now glitters with colors
This memory of conjugation got stored
      in my heart as nectars.

Within you, in this same manner,
Pull me in always fresh and tender;

In this life, to-day, you made me to
      undergo on Earth,
Seemingly a series of multiple re-births.

****

65. My Lord, my beloved, my richest possession
[Pabhu aamaar priyaa aamaar parama dhana he]

Oh, my Lord, my beloved,
My richest possession ever
Companion of entire journey
throughout my endless life.

In you I find my satisfaction,
Still therein I feel discarded.
In you I find my liberation,
Still with you I am ever bounded.

I taste the extreme sorrows
and happiness with you,
In my life, in my death,
 I actually stay within you.

I may have many destinations,
But final destination is in you.
In the abode of your eternal love
You are my supreme spouse.

You belong to all, also belong to me
From your wide world, to my small soul
You do play your endless games
Always new and afresh.

****

66. Only by One Salutation-My Last Salutation
[EKTI NAMOSKAARE PRABHU EKTI NAMOSKAARE]

Only by one salutation, My Lord, only by one,
Let my whole body remain laid down for ever,
On the ground of thy [flowing] creation !
Like the thickest clouds of Shravana,

Come down the grounds by it's
                own delighted desire,
Let by my single salutation, the single one,
Whole of my soul be laid down,
   On the gate of thy divine abode.

May all my tunes mingled eagerly
                Into the unified oneness,
And put before you in my single salutation-
And thus, all those songs and tunes
 Do get extinguished into the Sea of Silence.

Like the pelicans do fly to the Manas Lake,
Similarly, during the days and nights,
Through my single salutation,
     Whole of my soul do fly past
        The great ocean of the death.

****

CHAPTER-12 : Denial of death
{Deaths are not the ends of the beings}

67. The Universal I [The I within me]
[from Parishesh -Book of Poems-1931]

Now-a-days, I often think, do I know Him really,
Who speaks,when I speak,Who walks, when I walk,
Whose art-work is that when I paint,
Whose tunes comes out of my songs,
In happiness and sorrows, days after days,
In my heart and soul, who appears in diverse forms.

I thought he is tied up with me,
All laughter and cries of my life,
Within the boundary of my body,
He is bounded in my all works and plays
I thought he is me within me-
Flowing with my life, he will end up with my death.

Why then it comes in my mind, in my deepest delight,
By the touch and by appearance of my beloved,
Again and again, I do realize His presence,
On the shore of fathomless ocean of sweetness,
He stands beyond me, out of me.

Hence I know, that He is not a captive
    within my physical boundary,

Rabindranath Tagore :The Death and the Deathless
With the grace of heroes of ancient legends,
Loosing myself in Him

I discover myself, suddenly,
 beyond the boundaries of time and space.
I am that one who is covered by His shadows,
Remains hidden in a corner of mine
In the history of the great saints,
We learn about His beaming appearance,
Ages after ages, I the verses of the great poets,
That great I was revealed to the small I that I am.
Covering the horizon, the monsoon breeze

Draws down blue clouds,
Rains do fall down upon me;
Sitting for long, I do think and enquired about,
This 'I' within me, ages after ages,
Took how many forms and shapes,
And how many names, took how many births,
and passed though how many deaths.

How many times, again and again.
From the past up to the end future,
This great indivisible one
Within only that man, in this solitude,
I wish to peruse that me,
Who is ever present every where .
****

68. My soul returned back to my body
[a physical RESURRECTION]

From within a deep dark black hole,
I am back again in the solar lights.
Perplexed I looked at me,
A fresh look with a fresh new eye.
On the theatrical stage of my life on Earth,
The consciousness that kept flash-light on, all night
Helping to perform my acts
with sorrows and happiness
Where did it wish to take me now,
At that side, where seems to be no sights of shapes,
May that be at peeping point of a new dawn,
On the gate of a formless sphere.
In between the thin gap of light and the dark,
Seemingly seen the hamlets settlements
in that unknown shore,
Still stringing are tunes in my nerves and veins,
The voice of the deep blue sky.
The uppermost or innermost meaning
of that voice and vision,
Are revealed to me or not, can't say, but
A tray-full of facts dress with rhymes,
I do hereby present to you in words .

....

১৩৪৫, ১ শ্রাবণ ; "Shenjuti"-a Book of Poems-1938
NB:- In 1938, Tagore was declared dead, broadcasted in
All India Radio and published in News Media, but he was
found alive thereafter. That Experience is stated by the poet
in this poetic verse. Read details in his biography.

69. THROUGH DEATH TO DEATHLESS-NESS

Sometimes by sudden flashes, that formless beautiful One,
Appeared before me, but even then did not like
to be caught by a full visual;
Suddenly opening the earthen doors, down in,
The mother Earth shows her secret room,
There lies an indicative shape of His divine abode,
Down under the Earth, lies there, a covered jar of nectar,
Sitting therein Hymns are uttered by the Springs
The formless One appears there,
But again with covers of the new-grown leaves.
At the end of the day, I failed to know, what happens after the death,
Whether any shadow of the rays of this life,
Beams up to color the sky of the sun-set time of any other world,
To create some illusory pleasure.
Whatever I learnt about life, it is enough for me
May it have imitation, but it has also exceeded all limitations
The end truth of Him is embedded in my soul,
And it knows itself extended and mingled with the whole Universe.
"वेदाहं एतम् पुरुषं महान्तं "-Upanisad,
[I have known Him, that Supreme]

" **I saw Him, I have seen'**-to say these words,
No tune can play, no word comes to my mouth,
That I am the blessed one, whom can I convey that,
My heart is flooded with the pleasures
of the touches of the touch-less one.
"तामेब विदित्यातिमृत्युमेति "-Upanisad
[Only by knowing Him, you can reach beyond death]
What ever is knowable, anything of that,
ever known by me any time,
Who does know and say me that-
In whatever I got, lies something not-got,
I am running behind that,
In an adventure for that unknown .
Still my heart is jumping up with causeless pleasures
And lost up in dancing on stage of this Universe ;
Through that tunes and rhythms,
I shall slip into liberation and escape the death,
through the passage of death .
****

99

70. THE ONE WHO IS NOT A MORTAL [AMARTYA]
[A Ephemeral Resurrection -of Poet himself]

It illuminated before me,
It's me, my body, in a body-less form
Tearing off all the cords
that kept it bound with matters.

Only a short of feeling of vastness,
Gushing out a pleasant flow of beam
out of some unknown depth,
It speaks only through the language of tunes,
And mixed up with rhythms and
fragrance of flowery Springs;
Through the wink-less gazing
towards the endless distance,
Get emitted whose signals.

This body-less body, filled with
beams of many mornings,
Who have fallen in love with the Absolute one,
whose name is not known.
Who is the dearest one among
all those whom we desire,
Crossing the sea of death, He wants to go with me,
Like a sweet-fragrance, like a melodious tunes,
as the absolved one .

****

100

71. I AM GREATER THAN DEATH

From a distance, I got conceived in my mind,
Turbulent terrible you are,
      Earth trembles under your fearful rule,
          You are a horror,
On the burst up chest of a depressed ones ,
  you burn your fire with high up flames .
Thunderous club of your right hand,
        pricks into cyclonic clouds
To drag down flashes of lightening
Fearfully came with trembling heart
              To stand up before you.
Your terrible stares created
        waves of imminent turbulence
        Came down heavily on me .
Shuddered my rib-bones
      Putting my hands across the chest ,
I asked, " Is there any thing left,
      Do you have your the last thunder ?"
        Came down the last blow.
This only? Nothing more you have ?
      Vanished my fear .
When your thunder was hanging over me
 I took it for granted that you are greater than me.
Along with your thunder,
    you came down under,
On the very land of reality where we live.
You have been quite a bit low, now.
   I had to shed out my all my shyness
      Whatever big you are ,
But you are not bigger than death .
"I am bigger than death"-
    making this last statement ,
I will be ready to leave this Earth,
       at that very moment .
       ****

72. Death is like a Solar Eclipse only

Death is like a Solar Eclipse,
Only covers exitances by a shadow,
Can't absolve the divine nectar of Life force
Converting life into inanimate ,
 I know that with sure certainty.

Priceless value of Love,
Cannot be totally robbed off,
Such a robber can remain no-where hidden
In any caves and wholes of this Universe,
 I am surely certain about that .

What I got so true, the truest true
The greatest falsehood was lying inside,
In the garb of deceiving disguise,
Such a Scandalous contradiction in the Creation,
Can never be tolerable in the Law of God.
 I know hat with full certainty.

All that exists, exist through constant changes,
That is the law of time and space..
Death deceives with his face of a total stop-
[mocking the end of the flow of existence]
In this creative world-death is not thus
true as a final end;I am fully certain about it..

I being a part of the process of matters and energy,
Through out this Universe,
I being a witness of that fact of truth,
In my universal me, that truth is truly tied up-.
And I know that with sure certainty.
 ****

Rabindranath Tagore :The Death and the Deathless
[A Poem of Rabindranath Tagore's- from "Shesh-Lekhaa']

Printed in Great Britain
by Amazon